Gratitude with a Pause

100 Poems for giving hope and happiness

Dr. Monica Nagpal, Ph.D

INDIA • SINGAPORE • MALAYSIA

Contents

8. MINDFULNESS

9. ACTION

10. LONG POEMS

Acknowledgements

I express my heartful thanks to my mentor Dr. Daisaku Ikeda, who is the inspiration behind this book. I dedicate this book to him. My gratitude also to my family who have always encouraged me and appreciated my work.

They are the ones who have listened to my poems and supported me to pursue my passion.

Preface

"Poetry is when an emotion has found its thought and the thought has found words."

– Robert Frost

This quote by Robert Frost absolutely describes the real purpose of writing a poetry. The poems in this book are a result of few thoughts that came when admiring the nature, few came when I became aware of each moment. There are also feelings of being overwhelmed as a women, feelings of a child. Having gratitude not for big things in life instead to be grateful always. That is the best way to live.

I hope the poems will stir an emotion or awaken a thought in the reader's mind. The reader will be carried away by the depth of emotions and will be transported to the scene of poetry.

I hope these 100 poems become the anchor for someone and they commence their journey on the path of gratitude.

About the Author

Dr. Monica Nagpal is doctorate in education. She is founder of hopeandhappiiness. She has co-authored three anthologies. She is a writer, a poetess, minfulness meditation teacher, parenting and happiness coach, inner image consultant. She is also an inspirational quotes writer.

Writing poetry has been a passion for her since childhood. Poems for her is the best way of expression.

Her poems are a way of motivating, sharing, and presenting the ways of society. She also writes shayari to bring out the emotion of love, which is the most universal emotion. She wishes her pen to be that tool which can bring about a positive transformation in the society and to enable the youth to bring out their best potential.

About the Book

This book is a compilation of poems that will stir the heart and soul of the reader. It will enable them to reflect on their life. These are poems of love, of inspiration, of determination, of courage, of compassion. These are all about being human. The author hopes that these poems will bring about a shift in the thought process and thus will bring a transformation in the heart. One emotion that will well forth after reading these poems is of GRATITUDE.

Do share your feedback on www.hopeandhappiines.com

Chapter 1

LIFE

1. Live in the Now

Every time I think about,

how of my death,

I focus on,

how of my life.

Every time I think about,

when of my death,

I focus on,

living in the now.

2. Life on Hold

Daily battles.

Daily Wars.

Broken houses.

Broken bodies.

Shattered windowpanes.

Shattered dreams.

Humans moving from one country to another.

The life is on hold.

3. Life Is No More

The house is no more.

The parents are no more.

The siblings are no more.

The friends are no more.

The food is no more.

The water is no more.

The school is no more.

Life is no more.

I only exist.

4. Ebb and Flow

The ocean allows,

It's waves to ebb and flow always.

Keeping its own essence intact.

Such is life.

Allowing us to be born and die.

Keeping the essence of life intact.

5. Build Your Own Life

Become the architect of your own life.

Build foundation of deep faith.

Build pillars of unconditional compassion.

Build walls of mighty courage.

Build roof of infinite wisdom.

Build floor of enormous resilience.

Build doors of absolute happiness.

Build windows of strong relationships.

And then paint it all with loving kindness.

Chapter 2

CHANGING KARMA

1. Death

We keep preparing ourselves every day.

Worrying about tomorrow more than today.

Regretting the moment that was in the past.

Awaiting the time that will come, and will not last.

We all are born and pass away.

We don't live the life.

The life lives through us.

For it we only make a way.

2. The Final Moment

The final moment,

the moment before,

the delete button would be pressed,

and our existence on this planet will cease to exist.

The final moment,

which is decided by,

how we have lived our life,

with regret or with purpose.

The final moment

have gratitude,

and seek forgiveness,

and then exit smoothly.

3. Transforming Karma

For every regret

I determine not to repeat my mistake.

For every challenge

I courageously resolve to win.

For every negative thought

I build confidence to defeat it.

4. The Treasures Within

Winds of adversity blew so strong,

So as to bend the grass.

Lightning of misfortune struck so hard,

So as to shatter the glass.

Who will stand tall?

To face this nature's fury.

Only that who can it's

Ego, greed and anger bury.

That who has

Faith in the treasures within.

Can surmount all struggles.

Of life and surely win.

5. Purpose

What is the purpose,

of having a purpose in life?

Purpose in life,

gives us hope.

Hope in turn,

brings courage.

And courage paves the way,

for new opportunities, to emerge in our life.

6. Seeking Treasures

Looking for compassion? It is there in you.

Looking for kindness? It is there in you.

Looking for gratitude? It is there in you.

Looking for hope? It is there in you.

Looking for love? It is there in you.

Looking for happiness? It is there in you.

Just look inside yourself,

And you will find the treasure of humanism.

Chapter 3

PEOPLE

1. People Empower People

It is people who empower people.

People with integrity.

People with character.

People with compassion.

People who believe in harmony.

It is these people who empower other people.

2. Path of Humanism

The dark clouds of

suffering and grief,

will give way to sunshine,

as time of darkness is now brief.

Align your happiness,

with happiness of all.

On this path of humanism,

you will never fall.

3. Who Can Enjoy?

Who can enjoy a sea ride,

without the waves and breeze?

Who can enjoy climbing the mountains,

without the steep path crevices?

Who can enjoy living a fulfilled life,

without adversity and challenges?

4. Youth

Youth, you have the passion.

Youth, you have the power.

Youth, you are the driving force.

Youth, you are the impetus,

for the dynamic development.

Youth you just need,

To be you.

5. New World

Spark in their eyes,

and hope in their heart,

youth have all the wisdom,

which they can impart.

Our conviction in them,

will build their confidence.

A new world will emerge.

when youth will take precedence.

Chapter 4

ME

1. My Time

What is my time?

Time, I have in this moment.

When is my time?

The moment I decide.

How is this my time?

Because I take action in this moment.

Why is this my time?

Because this moment is what I have.

When my time begins.

My life develops.

My destiny changes.

I create new history.

2. True Self

Angry sometimes.

Sometimes at ease

Chaos sometimes.

Sometimes at peace.

No one escapes these emotions.

So, no need to feel sad.

Believe in your true self.

And just be glad.

3. Lonely vs Alone

I miss myself.

when I'm lonely

because it is you.

who helps me,

recognise myself.

Because it is you.

who helps me,

see my weaknesses and my strengths.

Because it is you,

who helps me,

grow and evolve,

into my true self.

I am happy

when I am alone,

because then

I have you.

4. My Mentor

One who understands me, when no one does.

One who believes in me, when others have doubt.

One who cares for me, when others have left me.

One who nurtures me, to bring out my inner potential.

One who accepts me as I am.

5. My Friend

You, my friend.

I will not reform.

I embrace you,

as you are.

The transformation,

will come about,

as our friendship grows.

6. My Growth

I helped.

I taught.

I fostered.

I gave.

I encouraged.

And I thought I was doing it all for others.

I found instead,

that I had grown in the process.

7. My Aspiration

I aspire not the stillness of the pond.

Instead, a life state of calmness.

One that cannot be,

disturbed by any storm of adversity.

8. My Inner Voice

Why do I fear?
When I have to start,
on a new journey.

Why do I feel weak?
Before climbing,
the summit of my dreams.

Why do I disbelieve?
In my own potential,
to be happy and to win.

There is an inner voice.
That tells me to stop.
That scares me of the consequences.

That holds me back.
When I want to take that leap.

9 New Me

Clouds of adversity don't scare me.

Sarcastic remarks don't deter me,

from my goal.

I am fearless.

I am courageous.

I define my path.

I create my destiny.

I am always there for myself.

Chapter 5

SEASONS

1. March

Its name itself suggests movement.

This is the only month of action.

So, let's March, to create-

A world of loving kindness.

A world of compassion.

A world of equanimity.

A world of equality.

A world of happiness and joy.

A world of peace and harmony.

Let us March together.

2. May I?

May I be helpful.

May I be healthy.

May I be happy.

May I be hopeful.

May I be in harmony.

This is my prayer,

This may.

3. Rain

When it is

stormy and cloudy outside.

And the sun refuses,

to show its bright side.

When the birds hide in the trees.

And the leaves are as if freezed.

It is time,

to expect it will pour.

And your life,

will get disturbed, for sure.

Instead of getting hassle by rain.

Rejoice and do not complain.

4. Autumn

Sun is setting a bit early now.

Leaves from trees are falling now.

Autumn is setting in.

There is beauty even,

in letting go.

For giving this lesson,

to nature I bow.

5. Winter

The cold wind starts to blow.

thus begins the winter.

Nature takes a pause.

In dormancy it enters.

Replenishing the energy,

it grows stronger by the day.

If only we could also,

use the winter of hardships,

to gather more strength.

We could emerge victorious,

when Spring comes our way.

Chapter 5

EMOTIONS

1. Hope

Every sunshine,

fills my heart with hope.

Hope of revival.

Hope of abundance.

Hope of health.

Hope of security.

Hope of success.

Armed with this hope,

then I take action.

2. Uncertainty

Uncertainty is of job.

Uncertainty is of education.

Uncertainty is of health.

Uncertainty is of relationships.

Uncertainty is of life.

Still, I'm certain to be brave.

I'm certain to be humble.

I am certain to be loving.

I'm certain to be kind.

I'm certain to be compassionate.

Above all, I'm certain to be hopeful.

3. Happiness

We seek happiness,

from the external world,

always feeling incomplete.

There is nothing lacking in our life.

It is already whole and complete.

Just ponder and look in.

Happiness lies within.

4. Compassion

When, with voice of compassion,

we sow the seeds of inspiration,

in the hearts of every human.

The flower of kindness will bloom,

for sorrow,

there will be no room,

and the fruit of happiness,

will take away all the gloom.

5. Peace

We say we will,

fight for peace.

We say we will,

win battles for peace.

When there is battle,

there is only blood.

When there is battle,

there is no peace.

Instead of fighting and battling for peace,

Let us be peace.

6. Responsibility

It troubles me all the time,

and my heart bleeds.

When no one hears,

my persistent pleads.

When they ignore and forget,

our inherent humanity.

And forget that to save this earth,

is our responsibility.

7. Joy

I said,

It is not joy that I seek.

I seek peace.

Peace said,

I come.

When you let joy speak.

8. Pain

Why am I not able to forgive?

Because I fear,

I will get hurt again.

My trust will be,

broken again.

Means I fear pain.

I forget that,

when I forgive.

I set free my pain.

9. Remembrance

The tears may have dried.

but the heart still cries.

Their memories are itched in the heart.

and will never be wiped, even if we try hard.

Destiny has given us this scar.

And has taken them away, very far.

We long to hear their voice.

When has death given us choice.

We will miss each moment spent together.

But now we let them go, that is what matters.

10. Truth

Who dies?

The body.

Who lives?

The self.

Who suffers?

The one who is,

unaware of this truth.

11. Stillness

I don't seek,

the stillness of death.

Instead, I seek,

the stillness of ocean.

Which, though still on the surface,

has its undercurrent.

to sustain the life inside.

12. Lonely Together

Sitting in different rooms.

with our screen,

we are a family.

And we are,

lonely together.

13. Resolve

When I pray,

I resolve.

When I resolve,

I change.

When I change.

I win.

14. Dare

Dare to be different.

Walk the path untread.

Not to defy someone.

Instead to define you.

15. Have Faith

Smiles will adore each face again.

Have faith.

Eyes will again sparkle with hope.

Have faith.

Voices will again sing with joy.

Have faith.

The bells will again ring in the school.

Have faith.

Your goodness will create the causes for these effects.

Have faith.

Chapter 6

THINGS AROUND

1. River

Let adversity,

be the rock,

trying to stop my way.

I am the river of joy.

Gushing over the rocks,

eroding them,

as I find my way.

2. Clouds

The clouds of anguish and despair,

will try to,

bring gloom in your life.

You be the sun.

Rise and shine,

and let the light of,

your courage and confidence,

Illuminate your world.

3. Darkness

Darkness envelopes us,

as we close our eyes.

And when we close our eyes,

to discrimination,

to disrespect,

to dishonesty,

to disdain,

to despair,

to disintegration,

in our society,

the darkness envelopes humanity.

Time is to open our eyes,

and keep a vision,

of a humanistic society.

4. Path Less Taken

I may travel the path.

less trodden.

Still, I believe,

I will reach my destination.

5. Adversity

The untempered iron melts in fire.

As strong and hard it may be.

A tempered iron withstands all heat.

Becoming a forged sword for all to see.

Every adversity comes to forge us.

To mould us into a stronger me.

6. Friend or Foe

Are you my friend,

or my foe.

I detest you,

when my progress is slow.

I seek your company,

when I need to grow.

7. Media

When I write my truth,

I hide yours.

When you write your truth,

you may hide mine.

When we together write the truth,

there is peace.

And absolute truth will prevail.

8. School

It is not about the buildings.

Neither it is about the classrooms.

Books don't matter either.

Nor do the playgrounds.

School is and will be a place,

where there are teachers and friends.

Chapter 6

MINDFULNESS

1. Blind Spot

Blind spots blind our vision while driving.

We have blind spots in our lives too.

These block us,

from seeing and feeling our core values.

2. Imagination

In my imagination, I discover.

In my imagination, I invent.

Every idea of my success.

I first conceive in my imagination.

3. How I Become?

What one thinks, one creates.

What one feels, one attracts.

What one imagines, one becomes.

4. Take a Pause

Take a pause to see,

the radiant sunrise.

Take a pause to smell,

the fragrance of a flower.

Take pause to listen,

the flutter of a butterfly.

Take a pause to feel,

the wrinkled hands of your parents.

Take a pause to say,

A word of gratitude and appreciation.

Take a pause,

to be in the now.

5. Today

As I start today,

today becomes past already.

As I think of tomorrow,

it becomes today.

I no longer ponder,

about the past.

Neither do I keep wishing,

for tomorrow.

Today is what I have always.

So, I cherish each moment.

6. Prayer

Prayer–
The ultimate power,
of the universe.
Prayer has the strength,
to breakthrough,
the heaviest of karma,
and illuminate,
the darkest of destiny.

7. Meditation

Not a solitary contemplation.

Not a passive posture.

Not a deactivated mind.

It is action with awareness.

It is manifesting wisdom for greater good.

8. What Is Prayer?

Prayer is conviction.

That this shall also pass.

Prayer is Hope.

For a better future.

Prayer is determination.

To bring change.

Prayer is action.

I shall bring the change.

Prayer is transformation.

I will be the change.

9. Creating Value

Alone I may be,

still, I can create value.

Transforming myself first,

I can transform,

conflict into trust,

division into unity,

misunderstanding into understanding.

And finally,

inhumanity into humanity.

10. Grace

When we are closer to the end,

everything starts to fall in place.

And if the struggle is still on,

do not fall apart.

Instead, accept it with grace.

11. Listen More

Don't stop speaking,

when asked to shut up.

Speaking is not only through mouth.

Speak with your eyes now.

Let your actions speak for you.

Let the sound of your heart speak.

Don't stop speaking.

Instead, listen more.

Chapter 7

ACTION

1. Being Creative

Creating hope.

Creating happiness.

Creating value.

Creating harmony.

Creating warmth.

Creating kindness.

Creating compassion.

I create more, because I love life.

And I want to adorn it,

With the treasures of the heart.

2. Behaviour

People forget,

what they get.

They remember,

how they felt.

It is our behaviour.

which makes the heart melt.

3. Diamond

The pressure of hardships,

solidifies me.

The heat of adversity.

moulds me.

The turbulent tides of challenges,

smoothen me.

Thus, I become a diamond.

Unconquerable and invincible.

4. Victory

In a struggle,

we either lose or win.

The final victory,

comes to the one,

who conquers,

from within.

5. See and Listen

With my eyes, I look around.

And still, to see I fail.

With my ears I hear.

And still, to listen I fail.

Only if I could see and listen.

And be more aware.

I would be more helpful.

And shall take more care.

6. So What?

You fought.
So what you failed.

You laughed.
So what with tears.

You inspired.
So what you suffered.

Remember you lived.
Even when death was certain.

7. New You

New will become old soon.

Another year will be gone.

How much you changed last year?

And how much you promise to change this year?

It is never about New Year.

It is always about new you.

8. Change

Change is what I want.

Change is what I need.

Change is what I desire.

Change is what I seek.

Change you forgot is not out.

When you change inside.

Outside will change without doubt.

9. Come Home

You have travelled,

to places of history.

You have wandered,

to places of mystery.

There are so many souvenirs of each travel,

lined up on the shelf.

But now it's time,

to come home to yourself.

10. Path Less Taken

I may travel the path,

less taken.

Still, I believe,

I will reach my destination.

11. War

In war

I don't lament,
my broken home.

I don't lament,
my broken body.

I don't lament,
my broken family.

What I lament is,
broken soul of humanity.

12. Fight

We fight to kill.

We fight to conquer.

We fight to annihilate humanity.

We fight to destroy the present.

We fight to sabotage the future.

We never fight to win.

Because to win,

we need not fight.

13. Illness

Illness-How I see it

Helps me be accepting.

Helps me be tolerant.

Helps me be appreciative.

Helps me be grateful.

Helps me be human.

Helps me to transform.

14. Five Senses

Smell until you embody.

Hear until you listen.

Look until you see.

Say until you speak.

Touch until you experience.

15. World Is Your Stage

Let no one snatch your smile.

Let no one take away your light.

Dance to your own beats.

Let world be your stage.

Chapter 8

LONG POEMS

1. No Time

There is no time they said,
for long conversations.

There is no time they said,
for long drives.

There is no time they said,
for having tea together.

There is no time they said,
for playing with children.

There is no time they said,
even to die.

I said life is beyond time.
So don't postpone living.

Because death sees no time,
when it comes.

2. Never Give Up

This is your time.

You have created it.

It did not happen in a day.

It is the result of each moment you toiled each day.

You fell, you bounced back.

You built yourself better, after each failure.

You lived your dreams every day.

And today you are manifesting it.

Keep striving, as this is just the beginning.

Just never give up.

3. My AI

I asked dates.

It answered.

I asked data.

It answered.

I asked essays.

It answered.

I asked ways.

It answered.

With its ability to make content

I was content.

Speed that could not be matched.

With the ideas I was perplexed.

All combinations were perfectly delivered.

And it totally left me bewildered.

And then I descended from my mind.

Down to the heart.

I just wanted to know.

How much it was smart.

I asked about the feelings.

It had heard the word it said.

And it took no time to answer again,

And it said my system cannot have this embed.

It will speak, it will talk.

It will make, it will walk.

It will help you build your career.

It will help you scale up.

But when you will have it all,

And you will need someone to share,

someone to care.

That is where it will fail.

You will be like a ship without the sail.

So just know this for now.

It is good to use it as a tool.

Use your wisdom and your mind.

Let it not make you a fool.

Let your heart rule the mind.

Lest in this race to win.

You will be actually left behind.

4. Alone

Into the sky
near the horizon
went my gaze.

I saw suffering.
The humanity, the society
crumbling.

Wait, Am I not humanity?
Am I not society?
Am I weak?
What can I do?

My weaknesses had
covered my senses.
I was not hearing
my heart.

The cries from around
had deafened me.

Then came a sudden light.
As if I was jolted from within.
The cries had faded.
The darkness was illuminated.

It was the voice of my soul.
It was the light of my soul.
The message was loud and clear.

The sun is alone,
and so is the moon.
It's always a single
ray of hope.
It's single spark
that can cause all the fire.
It's from a single seed,
that a mighty tree is grown.

It is a lonely drop
that traverses all path.
and builds an ocean.

You have just one heart
to love all humanity.

So, you are not alone
instead, all follows one.

Just move on,
and change the world.
Rise, rise and rise now.
and see the sea of humanity following you.

5. Freedom

Freedom is when

we are able to shun

the dogmatic rituals

of our respective religions.

Freedom is when

we are able to speak the truth

about the

vandalism in our society.

Freedom is when

we are able to

accept each living being

as having dignity of life.

Freedom is when

we are able to

rise above our ego, fears, doubts,

our weaknesses, and our insecurities.

Freedom is when

we are able to

guide our thoughts, words and deeds,

in the direction of humanistic culture.

Freedom will be when

we will be able to embrace the humanity as one,

breaking all boundaries of gender, caste, religion, state, country
and ethnicity.

Then and only then will we be truly free.

6. Thankyou

I could not hear,what you said.

The harsh voices of my inner storm

buried your voice.

I could not hear your silence.

Because to listen to your silence,

I had to silent my inner storm.

Thank you

I could not see your smile.

The sadness of my soul had blinded me.

That reassuring tap on the shoulder

just lifted the veil,

and stirred my being.

Thank you

I could not feel your presence.

The grief had numbed me to the core.

Only your prayers could penetrate,

the layers of my sufferings,

and bring me back.

Thank you

7. Drifting Sea Weeds

The drifting sea weeds

were not in a hurry to reach the shore.

They were happy

to be carried by the waves.

The speed, the direction

did not matter.

What mattered was

just moving with the flow.

What mattered was to be together.

The wave and the weed.

8. Story of the Seed

I was just got thrown away.

and the fleshy fruit was savoured and eaten.

The wind carried me, and I travelled,

sticking to the sole of someone's shoes.

My fate is always undecided.

Will I reach the place of my choice, or will I be left to die.

I am not afraid of the dark.

All the time when the leaves, the flowers, and the fruits

are basking in the bright sunlight,

I am hidden in the crevices of the fruit.

No light, total darkness,

hoping to come out some day.

And then, I do not get too many days of sunlight,

before I am buried again, in the darkness,

and left to grow in the womb of the mother earth.

And what a growth it is, I split myself open.

And I lose my identity, to give rise to a giant tree.

I lose myself to let my essence live on.

9. Do We Care?

When glaciers started to melt

filling the oceans.

We were enjoying the rafting.

We cared less.

When whales started to die

filling the beaches.

We were enjoying the suntan.

We cared less.

When war was killing children.

The land was littered with blood.

We enjoyed watching the news.

We cared less.

When the forests went ablaze.

Charing the plants and animals.

We were enjoying the new year.

We cared less.

When innocents were killed,

Due to someone's rage.

We were busy counting ballots.

We cared less.

And then a miniscule entity,

Emerged as a menace maker.

Stalling human life.

Annihilating without discrimination.

Do we still care?

10. Gift of Now

Every morning,

my heart fills with joy,

in anticipation of the sunrise.

How will it look today?

No two days has it looked the same.

Neither has sky greeted it in the same way every day.

Life gives us,

a new experience every day.

Good or bad is what we make it.

If only we could,

say yes to it.

And fill our heart with gratitude.

Each experience would turn,

into a gift of now.

11. My Home

I may swim to reach,

farthest of the shores,

but my heart will be anchored in my home.

I may climb to reach,

highest of the peaks,

but my soul will be grounded in my home.

I may fly to reach,

distant corners of the world,

but my being will be rooted in my home.

12. Hope

When you sow the seed,

and wait for it to sprout.

That is hope.

When the first leave comes out,

and you wait for the branches to be filled with leaves.

That is hope.

When you see the bud,

and wait for it to bloom.

That is hope.

When you see the flower,

and wait for the fruit.

That is hope.

When the tree has shed all leaves,

and you know that they will come back.

That is hope.

In our hearts we have always kept hope.

Awaken it again,

because

winter always turns to spring.

13. Being Humanistic

Me being humanistic

is to live not as a human being,

instead, everyday bring out my potential of being human.

To bring a smile on

each one's face.

To being mindful

and not think life to be a race.

To extend hand

of kindness to everyone.

To embrace all

without discrimination.

To make this world

a happy place.

Where everyone lives with

gratitude and grace.

14. Inner Transformation

For long I had been

listening to songs from outside.

It's time now,

to hear the melody of my heart.

For long I had been

seeing the beauty of nature.

It's time now,

to envision the beauty of my inner being.

For long I had been

conversing with my family and friends.

It's time now,

to have a dialogue with my own self.

For long I had been

having hugs and kisses from my loved ones.

It's time now,

to touch my soul.

For long I had been

working to change the world.

It's time now,

for my inner transformation.

15. Nature

The sun shone brightly,
illuminating every speck of dust.

The gentle breeze
caressing every being.

Birds gliding through the sky,
their open wings,
portraying the freedom of their spirit

Trees though stationary,
swinging their branches,
and rustling their leaves,
announcing their presence.

The clouds floating in the sky,
ceaselessly trying,
to hide the sun.

And there are unseen,

invisible creatures,

rejoicing the glory,

of the morning sun.

The serenity and calm

Unhassled, unbroken, unhindered.

Each life contributing,

in other's growth.

Each life surrendering,

to greater force.

Nature nurturing,

the soul of every being.

Gratitude is what we can have,

for this grace that we receive.

16. Spring

Spring is the season of renewal.

Little seeds sprout out,

after fighting the hard shells.

The sleeping buds bloom

and fill the air with pure fragrance.

Cold winter is not able to

stop any of them.

They use the harshness

of the chills, to strengthen their resolve.

They wait for the right time,

to unleash their full potential.

It is spring now,

and every flower,

spreads the message of joy.

Joy that is result of,

overcoming the challenges of winter.

Winter of life,

may keep you frozen.

Your heart may be cold,

due to the harshness of the environment.

Breakthrough the darkness of your limiting beliefs,

and let there be,

new dawn in your life.

Let the blossoms of spring,

fill your life with hope and harmony.

Let you be,

the spring of happiness,

for all humanity.

17. Just Be

Be the sun,

giving warmth,

not burn with heat.

Be the cloud,

giving rain of hope,

not darkness of despair.

Be the wind,

soothing the soul,

not uprooting the life.

Be the sea,

serene and pure,

not causing storms of destruction.

Be the rain,

washing away the grief and sorrow,

not flooding the habitats.

Be human,

loving and respecting all,

not judging and disdaining.

18. Moment

I tried hard,

to adjust the focus

the angle and the distance,

to capture that moment,

and as I clicked,

it had already passed.

I thought I would,

write the experience,

put to words,

the feelings,

but could not find,

enough words.

Eyes then I thought,

would do the job best.

Just seeing without moving a bit,

I tried to hold,

the moment in my eyes,

and still, it wouldn't stay.

Why hold it, I thought.

Why capture it?

Why put it in the cage of memory?

Instead let me surrender to the moment.

Let me be, in the moment.

And now each moment, lives through me.

19. Child's Plea

I don't need a toy,

when I cry.

I don't need an ice cream,

When I scream.

I don't need a chocolate,

to stop me from being late.

All this I do with one intention,

because I crave your attention.

I need your hug,

when I fear.

I need you by my side,

when things are not clear.

I need your trust,

when I fall.

I need your faith,

when I feel small.

You are my world,

Mom and Dad.

And I never want,

to see you both sad.

You helped me to begin,

my journey on this earth once again.

I will never let any of your,

efforts go in vain.

I want you to be,

my partner in this journey of life.

Let's walk together,

before one of us goes out of sight.

20. Who Am I?

I'm not my name alone,

I am also my behaviour.

My feminity,

is not my weakness.

My feminism,

is my strength.

It empowers me,

when I become more compassionate,

towards humanity.

I don't have to,

be like somebody,

to prove my worth.

I don't have to become someone,

to please somebody.

I am what I am,

a complete being.

A creator---creating humanity.

A protector----protecting the human in humanity.

A destroyer-----destroying the evil in humanity.

I am she-

S----soul of

H---humanity for

E---eternity

21. Being a Woman

When that boy in school,

hit me hard.

I did not tell you mom.

I thought,

you will think, I am a coward.

When that boy in college,

hit me hard.

I did not tell you mom.

I thought,

you will think, I'm lying.

When that boy who I married,

hit me hard.

I did not tell you mom.

I thought,

you will think, I'm wrong.

When that boy who I gave birth,
hit me hard.
I didn't tell you mom.
I thought,
you will think, I did not understand.

As I was growing up mom,
I had seen,
all your bruises.
But mom,
you did not tell me.

If only once,
only once,
you had shared with me.
You would have saved me,
all this hurt.

Now I promise to tell it,
to my daughter.
Because she deserves to know the truth.
The truth that women are courageous.
And the truth that women can fight back.

Reflections